OLD SCHOOL
GRIT

Times May Change, But The Rules For Success Never Do

Darrin Donnelly

Cover design by Damonza.

ISBN-13: 978-0692816424
ISBN-10: 0692816429

Visit us at: SportsForTheSoul.com

Sports for the Soul

This book is part of the *Sports for the Soul* series. For updates on this book, a sneak peek at future books, and a free newsletter that delivers powerful advice and inspiration from top coaches, athletes, and sports psychologists, join us at: **SportsForTheSoul.com**.

The *Sports for the Soul* newsletter will help you:

- Find your purpose and follow your passion
- Use a positive mental attitude to achieve more
- Build your self-confidence
- Develop mental toughness
- Increase your energy and stay motivated
- Harness the power of positive self-talk
- Explore the spiritual side of success
- Be a positive leader for your family and your team
- Become the best version of yourself
- And much more…

Join us now at **SportsForTheSoul.com**.

To Laura, Patrick, Katie, and Tommy;
who are everything to me.

And to all those "old school coaches" who
continue to teach life's most valuable lessons.

Contents

Introduction

The people who achieve the most success in life are not those who somehow find a way to avoid making mistakes or encountering obstacles. No, mistakes and obstacles are an unavoidable part of life. The most successful people are those who are willing to keep moving forward *after* making mistakes. They find a way not to avoid life's inevitable obstacles, but to *overcome* them!

In a similar way, happiness doesn't come from living a life free of adversity — a standard that is impossible to achieve. Rather, happiness comes from the contentment of knowing you have what it takes to overcome any adversity that will come your way.

With this in mind, it's not surprising that psychologists now tell us that the secret to a successful and happy life, more than anything else, is something called *grit*.

Defined as the willpower to persevere with passion and a sense of purpose, *grit* is what matters most in whether a person succeeds or fails. Numerous studies confirm that when it comes to achievement, *grit* is the difference-maker. Contrary to popular opinion, even a person's IQ, talent, and upbringing takes a backseat to *grit* on the road to achieving one's goals.

Dr. Angela Duckworth, the brilliant psychologist, neuroscientist, author, and Ivy League professor, has been a leading voice on the power of grit. Her vast research is endlessly fascinating and I recommend her work to everyone. One of her many studies on grit stood out to me as particularly interesting. It found that those who were born into the Greatest Generation were much grittier than members of the generations that followed, with today's youngest generation coming in at the bottom of the Grit Scale as the least gritty.

In her book, *Grit: The Power of Passion and Perseverance*, Duckworth states that when an older colleague of hers saw these results, he responded by saying, "I knew it! I've been teaching the same undergraduates the same course at the same university for decades. And I'll tell you, they just don't work as hard these days as they used to!"

While one could certainly make the argument that grit grows with age, most of us would agree that those older, wiser, and tougher members of the Greatest Generation are prime examples of what it means to persevere, to never back down, and to make sacrifices for a greater purpose. We could all use more of the *old school grit* they embraced.

The book that follows is a handbook on how to harness the power of grit. It's a rulebook for how to become a grittier person and overcome life's ongoing challenges. If you follow these rules, you'll be grittier and, thus, more successful in life.

The idea for this book evolved from a classic "what if" scenario. What if your archetypal "old school coach" — a guy who was born into the Greatest Generation and raised in the 1950s, a guy who had plenty of success throughout his coaching career but is now thought of as someone who time has passed by, a guy who is considered too demanding and too old fashioned to continue coaching today's young people — what if this old school college basketball coach found out he didn't have long to live? What grandfatherly wisdom would he want to leave behind? What lessons would he want to give the younger generation about how to achieve their dreams? If there was no filter on his words, what rules would he want to share after a lifetime of coaching, teaching, and parenting? And what if he decided to share these rules through a series of letters written to his grandchildren during the final weeks of his final season as a coach?

That's who Bob Flanagan is and that's the scenario this book explores.

Coach Flanagan is the voice of grit. He's a composite figure of several legendary coaches who are often referred to as "old school."

He's definitely a believer in John Wooden's old-fashioned values and morals. He's got Mike Ditka's no-nonsense persona. He shares Mike Krzyzewski's traditional views on the importance of teamwork, sacrifice, and education. Like Lou Holtz, he manages to combine can-do optimism with strict discipline. And finally, Coach Flanagan comes from the school of Vince Lombardi, where a no-excuses, high-expectations, never-back-down attitude is the coach's standard.

Bob Flanagan is a man with decades of hard-earned wisdom on what it takes to be successful. The rules he shares are honest and unfiltered. He's certain that while times may change, the rules for success never do.

If life isn't going the way you want it to go, it's because you're not following the rules laid out by Coach Flanagan in this book. That's the way he sees it and that's the way it is. Period.

Though Coach Flanagan's letters are intended for his grandchildren, they might as well be for America in general. This is a man whose timeless wisdom—once accepted as the norm—is in danger of becoming extinct for future generations.

Flanagan lives by the old school code of faith, family, courage, and character; and he believes too many people have gone soft these days. They give up on their dreams too easily. They whine, complain, and pass the blame. They spend all their time and energy trying to avoid challenges instead of bucking up and powering through them.

Flanagan's letters are a rallying cry for toughening up and building grit. Not only do his letters serve as crucial reminders of the principles and lessons that must never be forgotten, but Coach Flanagan's fifteen rules provide a clear path to success in any endeavor.

Consider this book an instruction manual for getting back to the values that truly lead to success and developing the type of old school grit that will get you through anything.

Darrin Donnelly
SportsForTheSoul.com

OLD SCHOOL GRIT

Rules for the Road Ahead

"It is not the critic who counts, not the man who points out how the strong man stumbles... The credit belongs to the man who is actually in the arena, whose face is marred by dust and sweat and blood, who strives valiantly...who spends himself in a worthy cause."

TEDDY ROOSEVELT, 26th U.S. President

My Dear Grandchildren,

It is with a sense of urgency that I write you this letter. Four weeks ago, a few days after my 74th birthday, I was diagnosed with cancer. I won't get into all the details about my condition, but I will begin treatment for my disease as soon as this basketball season comes to an end.

I've been told that the treatment will be grueling and that the odds of it being successful are not good. This season—my 43rd as head basketball coach at St. Rita's University—will be my last. I have to accept the fact that there's a good possibility I won't live to see the conclusion of next year's basketball season.

For the past ten years or so, I've had to convince recruits that I had no intention of retiring anytime soon. I told nearly every one of them, "They'll have to bury me before I retire from the game I love."

I didn't mean it quite so literally.

I'm not cynical enough to believe that anyone will celebrate the fact that I have cancer, but I'm also realistic enough to know that there are many who will be glad to hear that this is my final season coaching St. Rita's Knights.

I've got a resume that includes more than 700 wins, two NCAA Division 1 national championships, four Final Four appearances, and the highest career graduation rate of any active coach at this level. But, coaching is a what-have-you-done-for-me-lately kind of business and it's currently been six years since my team last qualified for the NCAA tournament. It's been 12 years since we last won a tournament game.

I've heard the grumbles. I've seen the look on my athletic director's face grow less and less reassuring about my future over the past few seasons. I've noticed a lot fewer warm smiles when I speak to boosters in the offseason. I've read the columns by local sportswriters who say it's time for me to go.

I get it. They all believe my time has passed. The world has passed me by. It's time for some new blood, they say.

Maybe they're right. Maybe I am too stubborn for my own good—and the good of the program. Maybe my getting cancer is a message from the Man Upstairs telling me he agrees with everyone else and it's time for me to move on.

None of it really matters now. Whether those who want me to retire are right or wrong, it's happening.

This will be my last season. Aside from my immediate family—my wife and your grandmother, Mary Lou, and your parents—only our school's athletic director knows the news. Nobody else. I don't want the news getting out. I don't want it to be a distraction for my team. If the media found out, every game would be a big to-do about me and my legacy. That's not fair to our players, especially the seniors. It's *their* team and *their* season. Not mine.

I'm writing to you because I have something I want to give you before I go, something that I know will make you happier and more successful in your life (a life that will go by much faster than you realize).

I'm proud to say that Mary Lou and I raised eight children and there are now twenty-four of you grandchildren. I'm so proud of each and every one of you. But I'm also worried about you.

You kids are growing up in a world much different than the one I grew up in and I fear that some of the most important lessons you need to know are being ignored by today's culture.

I came of age in the 1950s. We were raised by a generation of parents, teachers, and coaches who had survived the Great Depression and won World War II. They taught us how to be gritty — how to never give up and never back down in the face of life's biggest challenges. The rules they taught us were universally accepted at the time. Those rules, I fear, have already been largely forgotten.

People today think they're entitled to a life without challenges, but such a thing does not exist. They make decisions based on how they can *avoid* challenges. But instead of trying to avoid challenges, people should be learning how to *overcome* them.

~~They should be learning how to defeat the obstacles~~
~~that stand between them and their dreams.~~

In the weeks ahead, I'm going to write to you about the most important things I've learned in life. These are rules for how to live the most fulfilling life you can.

Follow these rules and I promise you'll have a rewarding life. Ignore these rules and I'm afraid life will be much more difficult and unsatisfying for you.

I suppose every grandfather has some "grandfatherly wisdom" he feels the need to pass on and these rules represent mine.

These rules are primarily intended for you, my family members who I probably won't get to see grow into adulthood, but please feel free to share them with anyone you'd like. I hope they find their way into the hands of anyone who may be struggling, who may be searching for answers, and who may care enough to understand what is holding them back from a more successful and fulfilling life.

These are rules that I've had to learn over a lifetime of relentless competition. When followed, these rules will make you successful—in any line of work. That, I am certain of.

They call me a disciplinarian. They call me impatient, stubborn, too demanding, and too strict. They say I'm an "old school coach" and that the values I think are most important are no longer relevant. The papers draw caricatures of me as the grumpy old man yelling at kids to "get off my lawn." They say the ways of the modern world have passed me by.

But they've got it all wrong.

The world will always be changing, but the rules for success will always remain the same.

I'm writing you because I want to share the timeless rules that lead one to a happy, successful, and purposeful life. Rules that should never be ignored and must never be forgotten—regardless of what anyone else tries to tell you.

I realize that the rules I'm about to share will probably sound simplistic and "old fashioned" to you. I know they'll only reinforce those characterizations of me as the "old school coach" whose time has passed. I could care less. I *have* to share them. You need to learn these rules if you want to be successful.

I see so many people living in fear, hopelessness, and apathy. I see so many people today who are too quick to give up on their dreams. I don't want that to be you.

Regardless of what modern society may tell you, the rules I'm going to share with you are the keys to a good life.

Embrace them. Live by them. Share them with the next generation.

Before it's too late.

Rule No. 1
Don't Accept Your Fate, Create Your Destiny

"You were not born a winner and you were not born a loser. You are what you make yourself to be."

LOU HOLTZ, National Champion football coach

Wednesday, March 4, 2015
St. Louis, Missouri

I'm writing this letter from a hotel room in St. Louis on the night before my team will play its first game in the 2015 Missouri Valley Conference's postseason men's basketball tournament. Tomorrow's game could be my last ever as a coach.

With a record of 17-13, we won't be invited to any national postseason tournaments. That is, unless we win our conference championship.

The only way our season continues is if we win. And continue winning.

That's one of my favorite things about college basketball; no matter what happened during the regular season, when the postseason rolls around you always control your own destiny.

It doesn't matter if you lost a few games back in November, if your team chemistry was a mess back in December, or if you lost your starting center for the month of January. Everything that happened in the regular season was building up to this moment. And now, you take everything that has happened to your team and use it to carry you forward.

The past is the past. Regardless of whether the past was good or bad, *you* control your destiny now.

That's exactly how life is.

You go through struggles, you learn new skills, and you overcome obstacles. You learn how to win and you learn how to bounce back from defeat. Eventually, you reach a moment where all those previous tests—all those wins and losses—are put to a bigger, more important test.

It's not about what happened in the past, it's about how you *respond* to what happened in the past. It's about the lessons you learned and how you're going to apply those lessons going forward.

If we win our first game in the Valley tournament tomorrow, we'll play again the next day. If we win four games in a row, we'll be crowned conference champions on Sunday. And with that, we'll get an automatic invitation to the NCAA tournament.

It doesn't matter that we lost 13 games leading up to this point. It's completely up to us to determine how far we will go from here. And that brings me to life's most important lesson.

If there's one single lesson I think people today are more in need of learning than anything else it's this: *YOU* control your own destiny; nobody else does. *YOU* are responsible for where you go from here; nobody else is.

If you take nothing else away from these letters, embrace that simple rule from here on out and you'll live a happier and more successful life.

I realize that virtually every teacher, coach, and parent from every previous generation has probably muttered something along the lines of, "Kids just aren't the way they used to be. They don't have the same work ethic or respect for authority as kids did when I was growing up." And while I happen to believe those things are true today, I fully recognize that my assessment is clouded by nostalgia — remembering the positive qualities of the past while overlooking the negative.

But regardless of whether young people today are actually less disciplined, respectful, and hard-working than they once were, I am absolutely certain that the most troubling difference between the student-athletes I currently recruit and those I recruited four decades ago is grit — or lack thereof.

People today are, in general, much more likely to quit at something than they used to be. They're much less persistent. Even if it's something they enjoy and are good at, they throw in the towel much faster than they once did. They're too emotionally fragile and easily discouraged. They expect things to be too easy and they get easily frustrated by setbacks. What used to be viewed as an expected obstacle or learning experience is now too often seen as an end-of-the-world crisis.

They view failure as something permanent, something that can't be overcome. They see it as confirmation that they don't have what it takes instead of an opportunity to prove that they do.

If a player struggles to learn a new skill or earn a starting job on the team, he's much quicker to request a transfer or give up the sport entirely. He comes into my office and tells me he's convinced, "It's just not working out." Or, "It just isn't meant to be for me."

It's amazing how much more often I have these conversations with players now than I did in the past.

And it's not limited to basketball or college athletics. You see it in all areas of society. People are faster to quit their jobs, give up on a business, or shut down a factory than they once were. People are much more likely to give up on a marriage and walk out on their families. People give up on their dreams much faster than they used to.

Where does this lack of grit stem from?

If I had to name one single source, I'd say it's the erroneous belief that you don't have control over your destiny.

Think about it. If you're convinced that whether you succeed or fail at something isn't really determined by you, then you'll be much more likely to throw in the towel and give up when things get tough—and let me tell you, things will *always* get tough at times. Why continue to work at something if you're convinced that your effort won't ultimately make much of a difference?

If you adopt that viewpoint, then there will always be somebody to blame for why you didn't achieve what you originally set out to achieve. There will always be an excuse for why you couldn't do this or that.

People blame their parents, their teachers, their coaches, their bosses, their teammates, their coworkers, their employees, their politicians, and their upbringings. If Little Johnny gets in trouble at school, parents blame the teacher. If so-and-so doesn't achieve this or that, it must be because they're unlucky or because the deck is unfairly stacked against them.

This fatalistic view of the world—the idea that your fate is predetermined and that you don't control your future—leads to endless excuses and people to blame. It breeds apathy and a "what's the use?" mentality. It's the definition of helplessness.

There are two important problems with this type of thinking.

First, if you start looking for excuses, you'll have no trouble finding them. And once you make it a habit to come up with excuses for why you *can't* do something, you'll never come up with all the reasons why you *can*.

The second—and most important—problem with fatalistic thinking is that it simply isn't true.

You *do* control your destiny. I've seen this proven over and over again throughout my career.

It doesn't matter who you are or where you come from, those who achieve greatness are those who *decide* to achieve greatness.

They encounter setbacks just like everyone else. They run into "unlucky" circumstances. They face tragedies just like we all do.

The only difference between the achievers and everyone else is how they *respond* to those obstacles. They don't make excuses or go looking for someone or something to blame. Instead, they accept full responsibility for how they respond.

How you respond to the events you encounter determines your outcome. This is the secret to a successful life.

Don't fall for the lie that says your fate has been determined for you. Don't believe for a second that a difficult setback means that your dream wasn't "meant to be."

Instead, know that your dream *is* meant to be if you decide that it is.

If you decide to get back up, to keep fighting for it, to keep working and pushing yourself forward, you *will* make it happen.

But it's all up to you. ~~It's up to you to accept full responsibility for your future.~~ It's up to you to decide how you will respond to negative events. It's up to you—and no one else—to determine how much effort you'll put forward from here.

Your future is in your hands. Don't ever believe that it isn't.

Some people will justify quitting by saying, "It wasn't meant to be." This implies that the Almighty himself has stepped in and told them to lower their ambitions and accept their lowly fate in life. It's just another commonly-used excuse for giving up.

Here's the problem with that line of theological thinking. Let's say two people with the same goal encounter the same obstacle. One person views this obstacle as a message from God to stop chasing after his goal. The other person views this obstacle as something that God will help him overcome as long as he refuses to give up.

These are two people of faith who encounter the same event, but their responses to that event are vastly different. Which person do you think will be successful in achieving his goal? The answer is obvious.

I believe in God, I pray for his guidance, and I believe he has a hand in everything that happens to us, but I also believe the Heavenly Father does what every good parent should do for their children: he provides them with opportunities, guidance, and support, but ultimately allows them to make their own choices. Like every good parent, he wants to see his children take responsibility for their choices and learn the values of grit, courage, self-determination, and optimism. And I believe the choices we make have consequences, both in this life and the next.

When it comes to matters of God's will, I try my best to follow it and I try to accept the fact that God will sometimes lead me down paths I can't understand. But, I also tend to agree with Benjamin Franklin, who famously said, "God helps those who help themselves." He also said, "If it is to be, it is up to me."

There are only two ways to live your life. You can believe that your fate is predetermined and that you are powerless. Or, you can believe that you control your own destiny and have the power to change your future any time you want. The belief you choose to live by is the most important decision you can make.

Based on the decision you make, you will either passively let life happen to you or you'll actively create the life you want to live. It's up to you.

You know where I stand on the matter.

No matter where you are right now or what has happened to you in the past, your future is up to you. *You* create your destiny, nobody else does.

Rule No. 2
You'll Only Achieve What You Believe You Can Achieve

"I don't think anything is unrealistic if you believe you can do it."

MIKE DITKA, Super Bowl Champion football coach

Yesterday, in our first round game of the Valley tournament, our team overcame a halftime deficit to beat a below-average Bradley University team, 51-49. Earlier this afternoon, we shocked the No. 11-ranked team in the country, Northern Iowa, with a 65-62 victory. It was our first win this season over an opponent ranked in the AP poll's Top 20.

In the postgame press conference, a reporter asked me how our team had turned things around so quickly from a sloppy win against the last-place team in our conference to knocking off the second-place team in our conference just one day later.

"Simple," I said. "We believed we could."

Some members of the press chuckled and shook their heads. They wanted me to reveal that I had made some vital strategic change to our game plan from the first night of the tournament to the next, but we didn't. You can go back to the film and see for yourself. We played our style of basketball the way we always do. No coach is going to overhaul their offense or defense this late in the season. Oh sure, we knew who their top players were and what they liked to do on both sides of the ball. We adjusted to those things and tried to play to our strengths while minimizing theirs, just like we do against every opponent. Every team in the country makes those types of adjustments from game to game.

But the real difference maker was our confidence level. The belief we had in ourselves. As a team, we believed we could beat Northern Iowa and we did it.

Reporters may think I'm being glib and people may blow off this type of answer as way too simplistic, but it's the truth.

We went into that first game against Bradley not expecting them to put up much of a fight. And we played as though we didn't have to play very hard, especially in the first half. We didn't give maximum effort and it showed on the court. A late rally saved us from disaster.

But regardless of our performance against Bradley, we believed we were a much better team than what we showed. And our players believed they were a team that could beat No. 11 Northern Iowa.

The Panthers had defeated us twice during the regular season, but we felt we gave away both of those games. We gave up a halftime lead in our first game with Northern Iowa back in January. In our second game against them, just one week before the conference tournament, they hit a three-pointer with two seconds left in the game to beat us. Both times, we reviewed the film and felt that we should've won the game.

We knew that we matched up well and had a team that could beat Northern Iowa. We believed our team *should* beat them.

And earlier this evening, we played up to that belief.

That brings me to the second rule I want you to remember: **You have to believe in yourself because you'll only accomplish what you believe you can.**

If you don't believe in yourself, nobody else will.

You have to have the confidence that you have what it takes to accomplish your goals. As time goes by, your results will eventually match your beliefs about what you are capable of. It won't happen overnight and it isn't an exact science. But *eventually*, you'll end up with whatever you believe you deserve.

Back when I was a young assistant coach in 1965, a colleague told me to read a book called *The Magic of Thinking Big*. That book had a tremendous impact on me. I still re-read it every offseason. One of the lines in that book was something I never forgot: "The size of your success is determined by the size of your belief."

In the 50 years since I read the line, I've seen that simple statement confirmed again and again and again.

It sounds so simple, but it's true. If you believe you're worthy of being among the best, you will act and perform as though you're among the best, and you will eventually *be* among the best.

It doesn't happen instantly and you can't lie to yourself. You have to truly believe—deep in your soul— that you've paid the price and are deserving of the success you want to achieve. But it's a fact that I've seen confirmed again and again throughout my career: **the best believe they're the best** *before* **they actually prove they're the best. Your results** *follow* **your beliefs; it's not the other way around.**

I've coached the St. Rita's basketball team for 42 seasons prior to this one and only twice did we win all of our postseason games. We were the NCAA Division 1 national champions in 1977 and 1986. Were those the most talented teams I've ever coached? They were not.

Obviously, players are quicker, faster, and more talented overall these days than they were in previous decades, but even adjusting for the different periods, I don't think my '77 and '86 teams were more talented than a dozen or so of my other teams—including my current team.

What those two teams had more of compared to all my other teams was strong senior leadership, tight-knit camaraderie, and *huge* confidence. They believed they had put in more work and preparation than anyone else in the country and therefore *deserved* to be champions.

They faced setbacks along the way. My 1977 team rose to No. 4 in the national rankings before losing their final two games of the regular season and then getting beat in the first round of our conference tournament. After three-straight losses, many speculated that our season was unraveling. But the players refused to believe that.

Some of those players were even criticized by the media for "making excuses" about why they lost those three games. But they weren't making excuses; they were stating what they believed were facts about why the best team in the country — in their eyes — had inexplicably lost three-straight games in February. They believed they were the best team in the nation and that something strange and unique must have occurred in order for them to be defeated.

They played up to that belief by beating every opponent they faced in the NCAA tournament. They believed they were the best and they proved it.

My 1986 team also faced plenty of setbacks. After a 3-3 start to the season and having one of our most-talented players suffer a season-ending knee injury, most people had written us off for the year. But not our players. Especially the seniors, who had put in four long years of hard work and preparation for this moment. They were *convinced* they were a team of destiny. More so than any other team I've coached, that 1986 team simply *refused* to believe they were anything less than a national championship team. I'm still amazed when I think back on the level of confidence they had in themselves.

They played up to that confidence level by winning 33-straight games and finishing the season as national champions.

Both those teams refused to let past setbacks redefine their beliefs about what they were capable of.

I'm convinced that as the ups and downs of a season play out, more often than not, the team that most believes it deserves to be champions usually ends up becoming champions.

Are there exceptions and unique circumstances that sometimes prevent that from happening? Sure. Bad breaks happen to even the most confident teams and when they happen in the tournament, it's the end of your season. That's the way sports go; the seasons aren't endless.

But in life, over a long period of time, you always end up achieving whatever it is you believe you will achieve.

Here's the most important thing to understand: **your life will move in the direction of your thoughts and you'll never achieve more than you believe you can.**

If you believe you're average, you'll be average. If you believe your goals are unrealistic, they will be. If you believe a past setback means your dream isn't meant to be, you'll prove yourself right.

We all have an amazing ability to prove whatever it is we believe about ourselves.

I can't promise you that if you always believe you're going to win, you'll win every game. That's not how life works. There are many factors that play into short-term results.

What I can promise you is that the more you believe in yourself and your capabilities, the higher you will climb. The more convinced you are that previous setbacks are only setups for your future success, the more successful you will be. The more you believe that you have what it takes to make your biggest dreams come true, the more likely it is you will prove yourself right.

You may be wondering where I think my current team stands. Do they have the confidence level to win a championship?

I can't say for sure. Like most things in life, confidence ebbs and flows through changing events. What I can say is that I've seen our confidence consistently build throughout the year. Right now, our players have a level of confidence I haven't seen at St. Rita's in at least 15 years. I don't know exactly how far this team will go, but I do know they believe they deserve to win a conference championship. They believe they're playing better, smarter basketball right now than anyone else in our conference. We shall see if they prove themselves right…

Rule No. 3
Embrace the Pressure

"The ability to handle pressure is all in how you look at it. I look at being put under pressure as an opportunity to show how strong and capable you and your team really are."

MIKE KRZYZEWSKI, National Champion basketball coach

Saturday, March 7, 2015
St. Louis, Missouri

In our semifinal game of the Valley tournament, we got scorching hot from beyond the three-point line and pulled away from Loyola Chicago to win, 70-53. We will now be playing in the Valley conference championship tomorrow afternoon. We'll be facing Wichita State, the No. 8-ranked team in the nation.

After the game, several reporters wanted to know how our team planned to handle the pressure of playing in a game where so much was at stake. After all, a victory would earn us a trip back to the NCAA tournament for the first time in six years.

"The pressure makes us play better," I said. "It always has. My program is built on teaching our kids to handle the pressure of big-time basketball. If I've done my job, we'll play up to the pressure on Sunday."

Most people today have a tendency to run from pressure. They cower in the face of pressure. When there's a lot at stake, they look to pass the buck to someone else. When things aren't going their way, their instinct is to quit or blame someone else for their problems. When the heat gets turned up, they call whoever will listen and complain about all the bad breaks and stress in their life.

One thing I love about sports is that they force you to face pressure head-on. The bigger the game, the bigger you need to step up.

All through my coaching career, I've made it a point to teach my players to embrace the pressure. Not to run from it. I wanted them to excel in high-stakes situations. I wanted them to actually enjoy the pressure.

That's right, *enjoy* the pressure. How crazy that concept is to most people these days.

And that's the rule I want to talk about here: **Embrace the pressure, don't run from it.**

Society today urges you to avoid pressure at all costs. Well-intentioned people tell you to avoid anything that might make you feel stressed or overwhelmed.

But the problem is that ~~the more you try to avoid pressure, the harder it is to deal with it when it comes your way—and it will always come your way. You can't run from pressure, it will eventually find you. If you learn to *embrace* the pressure, it won't bog you down when it inevitably shows up; it will push you to a higher level~~.

I've seen many talented basketball players who could have achieved greatness, but they always buckled under pressure. They never wanted to be the guy taking that final shot. They played quieter, with more timidity, when the game got closer down the stretch.

The best players I've ever coached weren't always the most talented; they were the ones who rose to the occasion. They were the ones who *wanted* to take that final shot with the game on the line. They didn't always make that final shot, but they always believed they would make it the *next* time. If the situation repeated itself in the following game, they'd be right there wanting to take the final shot again—even if they'd missed it that last time.

That's what it means to embrace the pressure. When the stakes are highest, you want to put yourself out there and lay it all on the line. Whether you make it or miss it, you want to see what you've got.

Michael Jordan was the best I ever saw at embracing pressure. It's no coincidence that he was also the greatest basketball player to ever play the game. He once said about taking the big shot, "If it turns out that my best isn't good enough, then at least I'll never be able to look back and say I was too afraid to try."

That's the attitude you have to have.

Every season, I conduct multiple practices where we'll suddenly stop what we're doing and tell our starters they are down by 15 points with five minutes left to play. I borrowed this drill from Dean Smith, the legendary North Carolina coach. The first time my players go through this drill, they have a frantic look in their eyes, they take panicked shots, they make bad passes, and they turn the ball over. But the more they go through this drill throughout the year, the better they perform in high-pressure situations. Eventually, they get to the point where they often overcome the deficit and retake the lead in this drill by playing smarter and more confidently during intense moments.

This drill, once a source of panic for my players, becomes one of their favorite drills. They have *fun* playing in a high-intensity situation with the game on the line. This transfers to how they perform in those types of situations during a real game.

The point is, you can teach yourself to embrace and enjoy the pressure. You can prepare yourself for high-pressure situations. You can visualize a moment of crisis or something major on the line and see yourself rising to the occasion and solving the problem.

Like all the rules I'm sharing with you, *embrace the pressure* is one that goes well beyond basketball.

The CEO of a company has to be at his best when the company goes into crisis mode. He can't pass the buck to anyone else.

Anyone can be a good parent who is always there for his kids when they're doing well in school, money is no worry at home, and everything is going your way at work. But to be a great parent, you need to be loving, supportive, and attentive even when your child is struggling at school, you're going through a financial crisis, or you're worried about a catastrophe at work.

It's easy to make sales when you're on a hot streak and you're exuding a natural attitude of confidence and cheerfulness. But the top salesmen are those who can still make their presentations without showing fear and desperation when they're on a brutal losing streak and unsure how they're going to cover this month's mortgage payment.

The key is all in how you talk to yourself.

If you listen to everyone around you telling you how you need to give yourself a break and avoid these stressful situations, you're going to buckle in the face of pressure.

Instead, you need to tell yourself, "I'm at my best when the pressure turns up." Or, "This moment is making me stronger and I'm going to prove myself to the world."

When you think like that, you'll start to view high-pressure situations as positive events, not negative ones. You'll recognize that the pressure makes you stronger, smarter, sharper, and more resilient. You won't spend your life trying to avoid pressure; you'll learn to embrace it.

This mindset will give you a tremendous advantage over everyone else around you.

While most people will spend their life looking for shortcuts and the easy way out, you'll step up when the going gets tough. You'll be the one people depend on. You'll achieve much more success in life because you're willing to power through the most difficult situations while everyone else is trying to avoid them.

Not only that, but you won't waste time worrying about the pressure that might be coming your way in the future. So many people waste so much time and energy worrying about things that might go wrong in the future. That's really what stress is. It's excessive worrying about what the future might hold.

If you believe in yourself and teach yourself to embrace the pressure that comes your way, you'll know that you can handle it. If you know you can handle it, then there's no reason to worry about it.

Rule No. 4
Finish Strong

"The measure of who we are is how we react to something that doesn't go our way."

GREGG POPOVICH, NBA Champion basketball coach

Sunday, March 8, 2015
Kansas City, Missouri

In the locker room prior to our Missouri Valley Conference championship game against No. 8 Wichita State, I wrote two words on the whiteboard in front of my players: *Finish Strong*.

"It's easy to start strong," I told them. "Everybody can start strong. Whether it's a season or a game, everyone starts off excited, positive, and enthusiastic. Everyone starts off full of energy and optimism. But fellas, after more than four decades of coaching, I've learned that while everybody starts strong, only champions *finish* strong."

It's a fact of life I've seen hammered home over my many years as a coach: **things are usually toughest right before a breakthrough moment**.

Just when the pressure is at its highest, when the odds seem most stacked against you, when everything seems to be going your opponent's way, right when you think you can't take anymore and you question whether it's time to throw in the towel and find something else to do with your life; *that's* the moment right before a breakthrough happens.

Maybe it's all part of a bigger life plan that we don't fully understand. Maybe we're supposed to go through one final test before we prove that we're worthy of a goal. I don't know exactly why it happens. All I know is that it does happen. Again and again.

In the spring of 1976, after four mediocre seasons as head coach at St. Rita's, I thought about quitting. I questioned whether I really had what it took. I felt we had the players to be much better than we were, but I couldn't understand why they weren't playing up to that level, especially at the end of the season. My 1976 team was the most talented team I'd coached up to that point, but they lost six of their last seven games and plummeted out of contention for an NCAA tournament bid.

That offseason, my athletic director told me they could not extend my contract past the following year. This reinforced my self-doubt. I was worried about my future and wondered if I was better-suited for a more "secure" line of work. I talked to my wife, Mary Lou, about resigning. God bless her, she talked me out of it.

The next season, as I mentioned before, my 1977 team rose to No. 4 in the national rankings before losing three-straight games in February. *Here we go again*, I thought to myself.

But once that team entered the tournament, there was no stopping them. When it was all said and done, they were crowned national champions.

I could give you dozens of other similar examples from my career and the careers of so many of my players. Just when things looked like they were slipping away, huge victories followed.

Knowing that things are often toughest right before a breakthrough reminds you to stay gritty. It's easier to stick with a goal when you know in advance that you'll need to overcome some type of crisis right before you achieve it.

It is life's way of asking you, "Are you sure you want this? Are you sure this goal is that important to you?"

When you can answer *YES!* by making the choice to power forward and refusing to give up, breakthroughs occur.

Earlier this afternoon, we played one of the sharpest games I've seen our kids play in years. As North Carolina legend Dean Smith always told his teams to do, we played hard, we played smart, and we played together. We controlled the first 57 minutes of the game.

With three minutes left, we had an 11-point lead over the No. 8-ranked team in the nation.

That's when everything that could go wrong, did go wrong.

We missed layups, turned the ball over, fouled when we shouldn't have, and we suddenly started getting dominated on the boards and giving up easy rebounds. Our point guard, DeAndre Jackson, is one of the best three-point shooters in the country. When he's hot, he's unstoppable. DeAndre suddenly went ice-cold during the final five minutes on the game.

With three seconds left, Wichita State missed a three-pointer that would have given them the lead. But according to the referee, we fouled their shooter.

It was a terrible call, in my completely-unbiased opinion.

The Wichita State shooter stepped to the line to shoot three free throws. He made the first two, missed the last one. We finally caught a break and the game went into overtime.

As I regrouped my team prior to overtime, here's what I said: "I told you this before the game and I'm telling you this now. Things are often the hardest right before a breakthrough. Things often feel their worst, right before you achieve something big. *This* is one of those moments. This is one of the moments where most people back down and quit, but champions rise to the occasion and conquer. Anybody can start strong, but champions *finish* strong!"

I saw light bulbs go on for my players. It hit them that they were experiencing a crucial moment, just like we had predicted before the game. This wasn't a moment of crisis that we were unprepared for; this was part of the process. This was how life worked. This was their breakthrough moment.

Despite the fact that Wichita State had nearly all the momentum going into overtime, our guys embraced the pressure. The panic I saw in the final few minutes of regulation drifted away and we played with confidence. We played smart.

When the buzzer sounded, we had knocked off Wichita State, 81-76. We cut down the nets and hoisted the Missouri Valley Conference championship trophy.

We were going back to the NCAA tournament.

Just four days ago, we were seeded as the seventh-best team in our conference with a mediocre record of 17-13. Now, we were conference champions with a respectable 21-13 record and two wins over Top 15 teams in three days.

Everyone had counted us out four days ago. Tonight, I heard someone on ESPN call us the hottest team in the country, a team that everybody better watch out for.

It's funny how quickly life can turn around if you keep pushing forward and expecting things to be most difficult right before they get drastically better.

You have to expect your most challenging moment right before your greatest victory. Remember this the next time you feel like you can't catch a break or you start questioning whether you have what it takes to accomplish your dreams.

Everybody starts strong, but champions finish strong.

Rule No. 5
Find Something You Love to Do and Stick With It

"It is imperative that we all make every effort to do what we love. My job is definitely a challenge, but I like what I do so much that it rarely seems like work to me."

NICK SABAN, National Champion football coach

THE IMPOSSIBLE IS POSSIBLE ONCE AGAIN.

That was the headline on the *Kansas City Star* sports page Monday morning. The picture below the headline showed two of our players hugging in celebration after our victory over Wichita State.

This type of play on words had been common back when our program was a national basketball power. Our school's namesake, St. Rita, is the patron saint of impossible causes.

St. Rita's University is a small Catholic college located in the midtown area of Kansas City. Mary Lou and I had both grown up on Long Island. We met in college and never expected to leave the East Coast. In 1972, when St. Rita's offered me my first head coaching job, I thought it would be a good stepping-stone opportunity. A place where I could prove myself quickly and move on to something bigger and better, preferably back East. Instead, we fell in love with this school, this city, and this region of the country. I've never left.

I've had good offers, believe me. Especially back in the late 1970s and through the 1980s, when St. Rita's was a regular Top 10 team. But many would be surprised to hear that I was still being offered quality jobs throughout the 1990s and into the early 2000s. Big-time programs came along and offered me more money and more resources. People don't believe me when I say this, but I never seriously considered any of those jobs.

Part of the reason was family. As my kids grew up, I didn't want to up and move.

Part of it was relationships with people and the community here. Mary Lou and I became part of Kansas City; the faces and places became part of who we were.

But the main reason I never felt like leaving St. Rita's University was because I loved what I was doing here. And if it ain't broke, why try to fix it?

My college coach told me, **"Find what you love to do and find a way to make a living doing it. If you**

can do that, you'll never work a day in your life." I never forgot those words.

Obviously, running a basketball program is hard work, but I immediately understood his point. If I loved the work I was doing, it wouldn't *feel* like work.

And that's the point I'm trying to make. What I've been able to do at St. Rita's has never felt like work. I love this game. I love this city. I love the relationships I've formed with my players, my colleagues, and the people in the community. Whenever those job offers came along, I'd always ask myself, *If you love what you're doing so much, why would you risk throwing it away?*

That's another problem I see too often these days. Everybody's always got one foot out the door. They're always thinking the grass might be greener somewhere else. They give up something they're enjoying and passionate about for the promises offered by new companies, new careers, and new spouses. The things they're hoping to find when they get there—like more money, more fame, more prestige, or more power — never satisfy them the way they hoped.

I'm all for experiencing new things on the road to figuring out what you're called to do in life and I don't advise sticking with a career or job environment you hate, but I think people today are bombarded with so many choices and so many messages trying to convince them that they would be happier with something else (or someone else) that it clouds their judgment. It leads to poor choices. It distracts people from doing quality work and enjoying the job at hand.

It's sad. People are so worried that they might be missing out on something better that they fail to enjoy what they're doing right now.

I've seen these stories way too often. People keep searching for something better and they never find it. All along, they should have followed their heart and stuck with what they were truly passionate about.

When I talk about following your passion, I'll always get a few people telling me, "But, I just don't know what my passion is."

I have a hard time believing that. What they really mean to say is, "There's too much competition in the line of work I'm really passionate about." Or, "I don't think I can make enough money doing what I'm truly passionate about."

Most people know, deep down, what it is that speaks to their heart. It was probably something they first showed a powerful interest in as kids or teenagers or maybe in their college years. But somewhere along the line, people started telling them it's too hard to make a good living in that line of work. They told them to be more practical with their life plans. They told them to grow up and get serious—implying that the passion in their heart, given to them by God, was something they needed to grow out of.

I understand the good intentions behind these messages. Parents, teachers, and friends don't want to see people they care about get discouraged by chasing after what they view to be impractical dreams. But I'm a firm believer that following your passion is the only way to make your dreams come true.

You see, **you've got to want something** *so bad* **in life that you're willing to make the sacrifices most people won't. That's where you'll find your edge. That extreme desire to achieve something only comes when your goal is aligned with your true passion.**

I've had numerous graduate assistant coaches through the years. These are young students trying to get started in coaching. It only takes me about a month or so to see which ones will make it in this profession and which ones won't.

The guys who have a love for coaching this game are the ones who show up early, stay late, and constantly ask questions. They're always looking for more information. They want to learn as much as they can. They can't wait to show up at work the next day. They could care less if they're missing out on some party. They think that coaching basketball *is* the party.

Then you've got the guys who like basketball, think they want to coach basketball, but quickly reveal that their true passion rests elsewhere. Their body language doesn't lie. They grumble as the season goes on. They can't wait to check out and they lose their focus. They're always wondering if they might be missing out on something better somewhere else. They stop asking questions because they fear it will lead to more work and they hope that nothing new is assigned to them. These are the guys who like the *idea* of coaching, but they don't have a passion for the process of coaching.

There's nothing wrong with these folks. I hope they find their passion elsewhere, I truly do. Because when they try to stick with coaching, it becomes a job to them instead of a calling.

You'll never be able to stick with and excel at something that is only a job for you. Whether you're in it for the money, the fame, the perks, or anything else, you'll never be satisfied and you'll always be thinking about doing something else.

But when you follow your passion, something that feels like your calling (instead of a job), you'll outwork everybody because it won't feel like work.

Oh sure, it won't always be a walk in the park and you'll get discouraged at times. But no matter how tough the going gets, you'll always be *consumed* by whatever it is you're working on. You'll never stop thinking about it. You'll always have this inner confidence that only comes from knowing you're doing what you were born to do. No matter how big the challenges you face are, you'll always have this drive inside you and this desire to learn more about what you're doing. You'll have this unquenchable thirst for your profession.

That, my friends, is what it means to be passionate about something.

Find your passion. Search your heart. It's deep in there and you'll only recognize it when you block out all the "career advice" you've been given by everyone around you.

Once you find your passion—your calling in life—live it to the fullest. That's the only way to develop the type of grit required to stick with it no matter what comes your way. It's also the only way I know to have a fulfilling life.

Rule No. 6
Keep Moving Forward

"The second you think you've arrived, someone passes you by. You have to always be in pursuit."

JOE TORRE, World Series Champion baseball manager

Wednesday, March 18, 2015

Portland, Oregon

I know that if these letters are shared with a lot of people, it will eventually reach those who roll their eyes and say something like, "There goes cranky old Bob Flanagan again, talking about how much better things were in the good ol' days." That's fine with me. In a lot of ways, things *were* better back when I was growing up.

As an example, here's a word that has become a disease for our culture today: *complacency.*

I'm writing this the night before our first game of the NCAA Tournament. All last week, as we prepared for our return to "the big dance," I saw something dangerous circling around my team. We were getting lots of pats on the back wherever we went. The questions from the media were about how nice it must feel to be back in the tournament. Questions about how surprised we must all be to have won the Valley championship. Questions about how it felt to prove the doubters wrong. Questions about how our players must have been rearranging their Spring Break plans.

These questions all had that "aren't you just happy to be here?" vibe.

I finally said to the media the same thing I was saying to the team, "Nobody here is satisfied with breaking into the Top 68."

My point being, 68 teams make it into the NCAA tournament. Getting into the tournament is a goal, certainly, but it's not all that big of an accomplishment. We want more. A lot more.

I hammered this message home to my team and my staff all last week and during our practices this week. We had to fight against the urge to be *complacent* or *apathetic*. Two of the ugliest words in the dictionary.

One of the rules I've most tried to live by consists of just three simple words: *Keep moving forward*.

That rule encapsulates two essential life lessons.

First, it means ignoring the odds. If you cower at the thought of facing long odds, you'll quit before you ever get started. My response to that type of thinking is, "Somebody's going to do it, why can't it be me?"

For years I've been told that St. Rita's was too small of a school, it had academic standards that were too high for elite recruits, its facilities weren't impressive enough, and that kids didn't want to attend "urban" colleges anymore. They said we wouldn't be able to consistently win against the big-money, big-campus programs across the nation. Even after 700-plus wins and two national championships, I never stopped hearing that one.

Keep moving forward means ignoring the naysayers and the critics. It means putting your head down and charging forward. It means that no matter what you went through in the past or what adversity is stacked against you on the horizon, you ignore it and power ahead.

It's like that old story about the general who brought his army from overseas to engage his enemy. As he gathered his men on the beach after their arrival, he had the ships they arrived in burned at sea. The message was clear: there's no going back now.

Nothing gets you more focused on a goal than having a mindset that says there's no way to retreat. You have to get rid of *any* excuse to turn back.

You have to tell yourself that you're in it to see it through. You can never back down.

The other lesson those three powerful words convey to me is that you must be committed to constantly improving yourself.

In life, you can only move in two directions: forward or backward. As much as people try, there's no way to keep things the same. As soon as you start trying to *maintain*, you start falling backward and losing your edge.

That's what complacency is.

When you adopt a keep-moving-forward mindset, it means that you'll keep climbing higher. You'll keep progressing forward and reaching new heights. You'll never allow yourself to grow complacent.

Once you accomplish one goal or reach one important milestone, you need to ask yourself, "What's next?"

That's what progress is.

I know some people may hear that and think, "But don't you need to stop and enjoy your successes once in a while?" Sure, maybe for a moment or two. But the fact is, the journey is always more fun than reaching the destination. Once you've reached your destination, you need to start a new journey. Otherwise, you'll get bored and…*complacent.*

I look around today and I see way too many people who are so quick to pat themselves on the back. They accomplish something and demand attention for it. They want everyone to look at them and tell them how terrific they are. They think that accomplishing one thing *entitles* them to everything. They start to believe they no longer need to work, to learn, to improve, or to grow.

What they don't get is that nothing is stagnant. Nothing stays the same. As soon as a boxer wins the title, a dozen other top fighters start working harder than ever to knock him off. As soon as the businessman gets promoted to president of the company, he better realize quickly there are a dozen other CEOs looking to take his company's customers.

This was the message I've been hammering to my team this week. What they accomplished to get into the tournament is nothing more than confirmation that they have the talent to be one of the nation's top basketball teams. Now, it's time to show the world just how far they can take that talent.

We're seeded tenth in the West Region and we'll be playing VCU, the Atlantic-10 champions, tomorrow. If we win that game, we'll play again on Saturday. If we win on Saturday, we'll play in the Sweet Sixteen the following week.

"There is no time to be complacent," I told my players today at practice. "No time to rest on your laurels. There are 68 teams invited to this thing; only one will be crowned champions. A lot of teams are just happy to be here. They think just getting here was the goal. That's not us. We're here to go further. We're here to move higher. We will never back down. We will keep moving forward."

There's no such thing as staying the same. At any given moment, you're either moving forward or moving backward.

Keep moving forward!

Rule No. 7
Put the Needs of Others Above Your Own

"Mental toughness is doing the right thing for the team when it's not the best thing for you."

BILL BELICHICK, Super Bowl Champion football coach

It's Monday morning and I'm back in Kansas City, writing this from my den at home. What a weekend we just went through.

On Thursday in Portland, we played one of the longest games of my career against VCU. It went back-and-forth for two halves and *three* overtime periods. When it was all said and done, we emerged with a 98-96 victory.

Our team had no time to rest. We had to embrace a keep-moving-forward mentality and quickly shift our attention to the next game. That wasn't easy to do.

Up next on Saturday would be Arizona, the No. 2-seeded team in the West Regional bracket. The Wildcats had won the Pac-12 championship and they were ranked No. 5 in the nation. They would be the toughest opponent we had faced this season. We were heavy underdogs going into the game and most people thought we didn't have a chance, especially after such an exhausting game on Thursday.

During Friday's practice, my players looked worn out. I overheard complaints about soreness and injuries. I saw sagging body language. I didn't see anybody diving for loose balls or fighting for rebounds as though the game was on the line. Our three-point shooting, which had become a vital part of our offense, was abysmal (when your legs are tired, long-range jump shots are one of the first things to suffer).

I knew there was only one message I had to deliver to my team before the Arizona game: *It's not about you! It's about your teammates. It's about what you're willing to sacrifice for the guy next to you.*

You see, our guys were exhausted after Thursday's game. At this point in the season, pretty much everyone is dealing with nagging injuries and sore muscles. A three-overtime game at this point in the year can deplete you physically and emotionally. It's easy to feel drained of energy. It's easy to let your focus shift to how tired *you* are, how much pain *you're* feeling, and how much *you* need a break.

But I couldn't let that happen to this team.

My thinking was that the only way to avoid an emotional and physical letdown would be to make sure each player on my team stopped thinking about himself and how tired he was. Instead, he needed to focus on playing for the guy next to him, his teammate, his brother.

Something magical happens to your energy level if you can make that mental shift.

It's amazing what a man can achieve when he takes the attention off of helping himself and focuses it on helping others. I call this principle, *The Power of Sacrifice.*

John F. Kennedy famously said, "Ask not what your country can do for you, ask what you can do for your country." What a powerful statement. A statement speechwriters today would never dream of writing in our "what's in it for me?" culture.

But what people fail to understand is that the moment you stop worrying about yourself and what's in it for you and instead start thinking about helping others and what you can do for them, you'll be instantly energized with enthusiasm and joy. I've seen this time and time again throughout my life. It's the ultimate prescription for renewed energy and it's the perfect way to get yourself feeling better when you're down in the dumps.

It's getting harder and harder to make people realize *The Power of Sacrifice*. Young people today aren't conditioned to think that way.

This brings me back to the lack of grit that is so prevalent these days. When a person is low on energy, they may not make a conscious decision to quit, but they end up quitting by default. Their effort and attitude declines right along with their energy level. They may not tell themselves they're going to quit, but their actions speak louder than words and they ultimately give up.

The fastest way I know to reinvigorate someone is to get them to stop focusing on themselves and start focusing on others.

One of the biggest differences between the teams I've coached over the past 10 or 15 years compared to the teams I coached during the early years of my career is that it's much more difficult to instill *The Power of Sacrifice* in my players today. They don't buy into it the way they used to.

That is, until this team came along.

On Saturday in Portland, we played at another level. We created turnovers up and down the court and somehow managed to upset the No. 5-ranked team in the country, 72-68, and advance to the Sweet Sixteen for the first time since the 1990s.

I believe it was *The Power of Sacrifice* that fueled us to victory.

Something magical happens when you quit thinking about how tired *you* are, how much *you* hurt, or how much things are going wrong for *you*. When you find yourself thinking like that, you have to shift your attention away from yourself and on to what you can do for others. Try it. You won't believe the results.

Our guys did that on Saturday. They quit thinking about themselves and instead focused on what they could do to help their teammates, their brothers, and their university.

When they did that, they played at a whole new energy level. They discovered reserves they didn't know they had.

On Sunday back in Kansas City, I found myself needing to take my own advice.

We were getting all kinds of attention for our return to the Sweet Sixteen. Hundreds of students and fans were there to welcome us at the airport when we arrived back home. We held a special press conference for the local journalists who hadn't made it out to Portland. And because Wichita State had upset Kansas in the second round of the tournament, St. Rita's had instantly become the talk of Kansas City almost overnight.

However, after the press conference, I found myself feeling down. Not because we won, but because life seemed so unfair.

Here I was, finally back in the Sweet Sixteen—back on the right track with my program—and yet, I knew it was all coming to an end for me. All the momentum we were building, which would certainly carry over into recruiting and next season's team, wouldn't matter much for me because I would be at home or in hospitals battling cancer all through the next season.

Why now? Why was the Good Lord pulling the rug out from under me right when I was getting this program back on track?

I'm embarrassed to admit these thoughts of self-pity, but when you get down and find yourself in a funk it can be so hard to snap out of it.

That's when I had to remind myself of *The Power of Sacrifice*.

This wasn't about me. It was about these players who had worked so hard to get here. It was about this university and all our fans who had stuck with us. It was about leaving the next coach with an overflow of positive momentum to carry the younger guys forward for seasons to come.

It wasn't about me!

I had to stop thinking, "Why me?" and start thinking, "What can I do for our players, this university, and this community?"

Once I started reminding myself of this, I felt myself straighten up and regain my swagger. I felt a renewed sense of energy and I became a lot happier person for Mary Lou to be around.

The Power of Sacrifice.

Maybe it's all part of God's plan for making the world a better place, but all I know is that every time I start feeling down, I can quickly bring myself out of my funk when I stop focusing on my needs and instead start thinking about others and what I can do for them.

I read somewhere that the two professions that consistently report being the happiest are firefighters and clergymen. It's striking that those are two professions where the individual must be relentlessly focused on the needs of others and how he or she can help those who depend on them in their time of need.

That's another thing I love about coaching. To be successful, all your attention has to be on helping your players get better. The moment a coach starts worrying about his job status, where he's going next, and how he's being perceived by the critics, he starts to lose his team. A good coach always keeps his attention on improving his players.

Imagine if everyone approached their job that way. Imagine if everyone approached their life that way!

If you ever find yourself feeling down, I guarantee you have let your focus turn inward. You've let your attention turn to what people think about *you*, why *you* haven't gotten the breaks you deserve, why *you* are not feeling well, how your family and friends don't appreciate *you*, or why *you* are not getting ahead.

The prescription for this is to turn your attention to others. Start thinking about what you can do to help *someone else*, start praying for *someone else's* needs, start congratulating *someone else* on their success, or start showing *someone else* how much you appreciate them.

It's amazing what a fast difference this will make. You'll get a surge of energy and happiness as soon as you make this mental shift.

The greatest coach ever, John Wooden, once said, "Oh, the great joy there is in helping others, perhaps the greatest joy! You cannot have a perfect day without helping others with no thought of getting something in return."

And that's what people today have a hard time realizing. They think that joy only comes from getting something for yourself. But life just doesn't work that way. The greatest joy you'll receive comes as a gift for helping others.

The Power of Sacrifice. It works every time.

Rule No. 8
Live for a Purpose Greater than Yourself

"A person does not become whole until he or she becomes a part of something bigger than himself or herself."

JIM VALVANO, National Champion basketball coach

The rule I want to write about today builds upon the one I wrote about yesterday. Turning your attention away from yourself and towards the needs of others is an instant fix for feeling better and generating more energy. It's a magical elixir for anytime you're feeling down. But you need to take this concept a step further and make living for a purpose greater than yourself the foundation for everything in your life.

Grit is the answer to most of life's problems. The rules I'm sharing with you are all rules for ensuring that you don't lose your grit—that is, your perseverance, your passion, and your willpower to never back down.

However, just telling yourself, "I'll never give up" isn't always enough. Grit needs to be a part of your lifestyle, your soul, and your approach to everything you do.

The rules I'm sharing are all designed to build up and reinforce your inner grit.

One of the secrets to becoming a gritty, never-back-down person is to live for a purpose greater than yourself.

You can be the most talented player in the country, but if you're not playing for your team first you'll never reach your full potential.

This concept goes well beyond sports.

You have to have a compelling reason for *why* **you're doing what you do.** This reason has to be a driving force that carries you forward when the going gets tough.

A paycheck isn't a good enough reason. Personal glory isn't a good enough reason. Proving someone wrong isn't a good enough reason.

In the short-term, these reasons can fuel you forward. In the long-term, they'll dwindle and you'll lose your enthusiasm.

You have to live for a purpose much greater than yourself.

It could a spiritual purpose. Doing everything you do in order to honor God would certainly fit with this line of thinking. I've seen more than a few players become great once they stopped playing for personal glory and instead began to sincerely believe that they were honoring God by playing basketball at the highest level they possibly could.

Simply believing that you were put on this earth to fulfill the very specific purpose of becoming the best version of yourself is undoubtedly a powerful spiritual purpose to live by.

Living and working for your family is another purpose greater than yourself that can drive you through adversity when things aren't going your way. When you find yourself struggling, simply remind yourself that it isn't about you and your personal enjoyment; you're doing this for your wife, your kids, your siblings, and your parents. Family is one of the most powerful sources of purpose.

I agree wholeheartedly with the late, great Tim Russert, who said, "When my life is over, there's nothing more I'll be judged on than what kind of father I was."

You can also find a strong, motivating purpose in doing what you do for your country, your community, your university, your church, and your city.

I happen to believe that what I do for a living serves several of the above-mentioned purposes. And throughout my career, I've had to remind myself often of those purposes.

The point is, you have to believe that what you're doing is for something greater than yourself. You have to believe that you're living a calling, not just a career. You have to believe that your sacrifices are for something much more than just your own personal benefit. It's got be for the benefit of others.

A purpose greater than yourself is essential to a successful life. If you're not living for a purpose greater than yourself, it's only a matter of time before you give up on whatever it is you're trying to do.

Rule No. 9
Eliminate Negative Influences

"The attitude a person develops is the most important ingredient in determining the level of success."

PAT RILEY, NBA Champion basketball coach

Wednesday, March 25, 2015
Los Angeles, California

As we prepared for our game tomorrow against Xavier University here in L.A., I was forced to answer questions about a story that was published this morning in *USA Today*. It was an article about Jeremy Dent.

Jeremy was a former player of mine. He was the highest-rated recruit I had landed in more than 25 years. Now, those recruiting rankings don't tell the whole story about a player's potential, but they do give you a sense of how much talent an individual player has. And Jeremy has an unbelievable amount of talent.

I recruited him out of Iowa just two off-seasons ago. His signing with St. Rita's shocked the nation. This six-foot-eleven center had offers from Duke, Kentucky, Kansas, Indiana, North Carolina, and just about every other elite basketball school. Most people projected him as a player who would quickly jump to the NBA after just one season in college. He told the media he chose St. Rita's because his father, who had passed away when Jeremy was a freshman in high school, had said that I was his favorite coach. He also said he knew he could start right away at St. Rita's.

But Jeremy didn't last long at St. Rita's.

As a freshman, he had all the physical tools and he knew it. What he lacked was the type of selfless leadership skills required to be a great player.

That didn't surprise me. This was an issue I dealt with constantly throughout my career. The superstar high school player always has to learn how to be part of a team. You can't blame them; these guys come into our program after being told how great they are for the past several years. In many cases, they've been told over and over that they are the greatest player to *ever* play at whatever school they come from. That was the case with Jeremy, but it certainly wasn't unique to him. Chipping away at the egotism of freshmen entering our program was a standard part of the coaching process.

In Jeremy's case, though, this process was harder than most. From the beginning, he believed he was doing me, his teammates, and our university a big favor by coming to our lowly little school.

As hard as I tried, I couldn't get him to understand the values of selflessness and playing for a purpose greater than his own personal glory. After summer and fall practices with Jeremy, I could sense that I still had a lot of work to do with him. I could also sense that he had become a toxic personality in the locker room. His negative attitude was affecting the entire team.

While I was certain Jeremy would be one of the top scorers and defenders on our team if he played as a true freshman, I feared that his attitude wouldn't improve and that it could do irrevocable damage to the foundation of our team. I saw that there was division between him and the other players. Jeremy seemed to resent having any senior lead our team meetings — as they have done for all 43 seasons of my coaching career — and he certainly didn't appreciate hearing any advice from his coaches or fellow teammates. Time and again, I saw him shaking his head at his teammates, laughing at them after mistakes, and blaming them for not getting him the ball where he needed it. A few times at practice, fights nearly broke out between Jeremy and the others.

Again, these problems weren't unique to a young player like Jeremy. I had coached several star freshmen through the decades who also had to be coached out of their negative attitudes. It just takes time. Some change their ways quicker than others. In Jeremy's case, I could sense this was going to be a longer process.

I decided to redshirt Jeremy for a year so that his negativity didn't spread throughout the team. I've coached long enough to be certain that attitude is contagious and I couldn't let Jeremy's negativity infect the rest of the team.

A week before the season was to begin, I told Jeremy I thought it would be best for him to redshirt his freshman season.

"If you redshirt me today, I'll transfer tomorrow," Jeremy snapped. "That's not a threat, that's a promise."

I extended my hand and told him, "Best of luck to you."

Jeremy never played a single game for us.

The media had a field day with the news. It played perfectly into all the things they'd been saying about me. The idea that I couldn't relate to young people anymore. The idea that my old-fashioned ways had run off our most promising recruit in decades.

But what the media didn't understand is that I knew we had a special group of young players and I couldn't risk letting one bad attitude rip this team apart. I knew from experience that negativity could infect a program and hurt it for years to come.

Had Jeremy played with us last season, he certainly would have put up a lot of points, but I couldn't take the risk of what that could do to the rest of the team. What trust would they have for me if I were to start a guy who essentially violated the values and principles I had been teaching everyone else since they arrived at St. Rita's?

I granted Jeremy an immediate release of his scholarship and he joined a new team in less than a week. He led his conference in scoring and entered the NBA draft after his freshman season. I'm sure Jeremy doesn't have very warm feelings for me today, but I wish him nothing but the best and I sincerely hope that he looks back some day and understands what I was trying to do and why I had to do it.

This morning's article in *USA Today* had a "what could have been" angle to it. The story speculated that had Jeremy Dent played on our team last season, he probably could have been convinced to stay for this season, and our team's postseason success would be surprising no one. It said that instead of being this year's "Cinderella story," we would have been one of the nation's most dominant teams from the very beginning of the season. They even had a quote from Jeremy saying he had intended on playing for four years and graduating from St. Rita's, "but I guess they didn't want me there."

When asked to comment on the article, I told reporters, "I think things have worked out pretty well for Jeremy and for us."

They pressed me with follow-up questions, but I didn't take the bait. I didn't need a story like this becoming a distraction.

The truth is, though, we're a better team without Jeremy than with him—assuming, of course, that Jeremy's attitude would have stayed the same.

Attitude is contagious and negative influences must be eliminated as soon as possible.

There are two ways to eliminate a negative attitude.

First, you can turn a negative influence into a positive one. In the case of coaching young athletes, this is done by teaching them *The Power of Sacrifice* I discussed earlier and the power of positive self-talk. Not every negative attitude stems from selfishness. Some people simply get too down on themselves after a mistake and this too can negatively affect everybody around them.

What you say when you talk to yourself is the single biggest influence on your attitude. Yet, most people give little thought to what they say to themselves. They say things to themselves that they would never say out loud to even their worst enemies.

Want to whittle away at your grit—your willpower to persevere at something that's important to you? Start talking down to yourself and telling yourself all the reasons something *can't* be done. You'll be looking to quit in no time.

You have to monitor your self-talk the same way you monitor any other behavioral habit. You can't talk down to yourself; you have to talk yourself up.

Don't let that voice in your head say things like:

"I can't do it."

"This will never happen for me."

"So-and-so was right, I don't have what it takes."

"Everybody else gets all the breaks; I'm just unlucky."

Instead, you need to be saying things like this when you're talking to yourself:

"I will find a way to make it happen."

"I refuse to back down."

"I will prove so-and-so wrong and show the world what I'm made of."

"The harder I work, the luckier I get."

Utilizing the power of positive self-talk doesn't mean you have to always be smiling and laid back. It doesn't mean you refuse to face reality. Most my former players will tell you I was a demanding coach, that I wasn't the most cordial guy when I disagreed with something, and that I may not have had the rosiest exterior personality, but every player I've ever coached will also tell you that I constantly stressed the power of positive self-talk.

I know the power of mental programming. **Our words have tremendous power and when you root out negative self-talk and replace it with positive self-talk, miracles happen.**

The other way to eliminate negativity is to simply cut it loose. This is not the preferred solution, but sometimes it's the only solution.

If you can't change it, you have to cut it loose.

If you're in a negative work environment that doesn't appear to ever be changing, it's time to find a new place to work.

If you've got well-meaning friends or family members who constantly bring you down, it's time to cut them loose. (This doesn't have to be a verbal confrontation, but you need to consciously block out their comments and purposely limit the amount of time you're spending with them.)

If you're reading or watching things that make you cynical or make you feel bad about life, you've got to cut those influences out.

This is all easier said than done. There's a strange allure that negativity has on us. We humans have an inexplicable urge to seek out bad news or align ourselves with easy excuses for not going after what will ultimately make us happy.

You have to be strong and avoid these negative influences.

Your attitude will determine the type of life you live. And the great news is, you get to choose your attitude.

But you must be aware that attitude is contagious. **Your attitude affects those around you, which is why you owe it to the people around you to build a positive attitude. And the attitude of others affects you, which is why you need to be aware of and cut out the toxic negative influences in your life.**

Regardless of whether they come from inside you or from outside of you, you must eliminate negative influences.

Rule No. 10
Effort Trumps Talent

"The difference between a successful person and others is not a lack of strength, not a lack of knowledge, but rather a lack of will."

VINCE LOMBARDI, Super Bowl Champion football coach

We beat Xavier University yesterday, 61-57. The victory advances us to the Elite Eight. St. Rita's Knights are now one win away from making it the Final Four for the fifth time in my coaching career, but the first time in 25 seasons.

We entered the tournament as the No. 10 seed in the West Region. In the South Region, UCLA was a No. 11 seed that also made it to the Sweet Sixteen. They lost earlier this evening. That means we're now the highest-seeded team still alive in the tournament.

Every year it seems that some team comes along and advances much further in the NCAA tournament than all the experts thought they could. In 2014, Dayton made it to the Elite Eight as a No. 11-seeded team. In 2013, Wichita State made it all the way to the Final Four as a No. 9-seeded team. These "Cinderella stories" are what makes March Madness one of America's most-loved sporting events year-in and year-out.

This year, we're that Cinderella team. We're the team that has advanced much further than the experts thought we could.

My youngest daughter, Marie, called after our victory and asked me if this was the most fun I'd ever had as a coach.

"Every year is fun," I told her. "The only difference this year is that I know it's going to be my last season and I'm probably trying to embrace the experience more because of that."

"But don't you take a little more satisfaction this year in knowing that you're finding a way to beat teams that are more talented than St. Rita's?" she asked.

"Talent is overrated," I said. "It's the effort that matters most."

And that sums up nicely another important rule that you should always remember: **In the long run, effort and perseverance always trump talent**.

Bear Bryant, the legendary Alabama football coach, taught me that lesson back in the late 1970s.

After St. Rita's won the 1977 basketball national championship and Coach Bryant's Alabama team won the 1978 football national championship, we met each other at some speaking engagements. We began a friendship that would last until his death in 1983. During the five years I knew him, we had many long talks about coaching and about life. The one thing that always stood out to me was how often Coach Bryant would pass up on recruiting a more talented player for a smaller, scrappier player that he knew would be willing to give more effort for his team.

"The ones who have something to prove are the ones you really want to recruit," he once told me.

My high school coach, a legend in his own right, used to tell us, "You'll find that in the game of basketball and in most other things in life, the more aggressive team usually wins."

I never forgot those words and I've seen that message proven throughout my years as a coach.

I don't mean to imply that talent isn't important. It is. Obviously, the players I end up recruiting prove that they are talented before they ever show up on our radar as prospects. But how do you think those players become talented in the first place? They got there by working extremely hard to develop that talent and excel at something that sparked their interest at a young age. That's the same way great writers become great writers, great teachers become great teachers, great business leaders become great business leaders, and so on.

I believe it's all part of God's plan. Somewhere early in our lives, he leads us to something we have a deep interest in, something we're really passionate about. Turns out, we've been blessed with just enough "natural talent" to pursue that passion. After that, it's up to each one of us to work extremely hard at developing the talent we've been given.

From there, it's your effort and your perseverance that determines how high you will climb.

Basketball serves as another good example. Once you're competing as a Division 1 basketball team, especially one that has won its conference championship and has advanced at least a couple rounds into the NCAA tournament, the difference in overall talent isn't as vast as some observers seem to think. Every team still alive has scholarship athletes who were stars from wherever they came from.

A clever phrase used often is: "Hard work beats talent when talent doesn't work hard."

I agree wholeheartedly with that statement. I've seen enough talented individuals who fail to live up to their potential because they didn't work as hard as guys with much less natural ability.

Effort is a lot like confidence. The team who has the most will usually end up winning—especially in the long run.

A huge problem I see today is people thinking that talent is some sort of set-in-stone thing. They love to label people as "natural" talents. They see someone achieve something significant and marvel at their "natural" gifts. This goes beyond athletic talent. We hear people talk about someone being "naturally" smart, but they never talk about the endless hours that person put into studying.

The problem with this type of thinking is that it implies that talent is something given to you and not something you have to go out and earn.

It feeds into a fatalistic, helpless way of thinking. It makes for an easy excuse for those who want to claim they just weren't born with so-and-so's talent and therefore don't have what it takes to achieve their dream.

A perfect example of someone who developed his talent is our team's current point guard, DeAndre Jackson. Here's an undersized kid who I recruited for his quickness, his ball-handling skills, and his defensive skills. But I told DeAndre at his first day of practice that if he wanted to become the starting point guard in our offense, he'd have to become a great three-point shooter.

This wasn't easy for DeAndre to hear. In high school, he had relied on his speed and quickness to beat opponents to the hoop and rack up lots of points. But I told him that in the college game, he couldn't rely on speed alone. He needed to be able to score consistently from beyond the arc.

DeAndre bought into what I was saying and worked every single day on his long-range jump shot. Before practice, after practice, even on days when we didn't have practice; I could hear DeAndre in the gym shooting and working on his footwork to create open space at the three-point line.

Sure enough, as a senior, DeAndre Jackson has not only led our conference in three-point scoring, but he's become one of the nation's top three-point shooters. He wasn't "naturally talented" as a three-point shooter. No, DeAndre worked his butt off to become a talented three-point shooter.

My point here is that **talent, intelligence, and skill are not stagnant things. You can improve at anything if you make a commitment to work extremely hard at it.**

Don't buy into that popular line of thinking that says you can't achieve something because you're not as naturally talented as someone else. Go out there and make yourself better. Make yourself smarter, grittier, and more talented.

Your effort is what ultimately determines your results.

Don't ever forget this: **in the long run, effort *ALWAYS* trumps talent**.

Rule No. 11
Focus on Only the Things You Can Control

"Being disciplined in your approach to each day of your life and accomplishing the things you dream of starts by disciplining your thoughts."

TONY DUNGY, Super Bowl Champion football coach

It's Sunday morning. Our team is on a jet heading back to Kansas City. I should be elated, but I'm furious.

Last night, DeAndre Jackson tied an NCAA tournament record by making 11 three-pointers. It was unbelievable. I've never seen anything like it. And I'm pretty sure Wisconsin, the nation's No. 3-ranked team, had never seen anything like it either.

Jackson caught fire about five minutes into the second half when we were trailing the Badgers by nine. During a 10-minute stretch, he hit 8-of-10 three-point attempts and led us to a furious comeback. He was an unstoppable force.

Jackson finished the game with 41 points and we won, 77-68. The victory punched our ticket to the Final Four.

I still can't believe it.

I also can't believe what happened in the press conference after the game.

After fielding a few questions about how we pulled off the upset and what it felt like to be back in the Final Four, a reporter from the *Kansas City Star*, our hometown paper, said, "Coach, earlier today it was revealed that this will be your final season as head coach of the St. Rita's Knights. How long have you known this will be your final season and who do you expect your successor to be?"

I was blindsided and the entire room gasped at the news. I'm sure I didn't do a very good job of hiding my anger as my blood boiled. I didn't want to blatantly lie, but I also wanted to wait until after the season to address this. I didn't want my retirement to be a distraction and I wanted to tell my players and my staff when the time was right.

As I glared at the reporter, I could see in my peripheral vision the St. Rita's players who were sharing the table with me looking my way. I turned both ways and saw their faces pleading with a look that asked me, *Is this true?*

"This isn't the time or place to address that," I said into the microphone. And with that, I stood up and walked out of the press conference.

I then met with my players and coaches in the locker room and told them that the news was true. This would be my last season at St. Rita's.

They were shocked. Some—especially my assistant coaches—looked angry, like they had been betrayed by me keeping a secret from them. I understood. I'm sure I would've felt the same way and I told them that.

As I continued to come clean and explain why I was stepping down and why I was keeping it a secret, I saw the looks of resentment slipping away.

I told my players, "Here's what I can tell you for certain. No matter what happens next week and even if we had never made it to the tournament in the first place, I can't think of a better squad than you guys to coach as my final team."

We had an open conversation after that. Hugs followed and some tears were shed. Then, I made it clear that it was time to get back to business.

"There are going to be a lot of potential distractions this week," I said. "There always are when you make it to the Final Four. There are going to be even more with questions about my retirement. Ignore them. Don't lose your focus. The teams that come out on top this late in the season are the ones who keep an intense focus on the task at hand. You can't control all the questions you're going to get this week, but you can control whether you let those questions become a distraction. You have to stay focused. You have to concentrate on only what you can control: your effort and your attitude. You do that and we'll be fine."

As I write this letter, I realize that I need to take my own advice. Here I am, stewing about who leaked the story and wondering why the reporter didn't approach me quietly to ask me about it.

Yet, these are things I can't do anything about. The past is the past and there's nothing I can change about it.

What I can do is turn my focus to the task at hand. I must shift my attention to how we prepare for our next game, which will be against the undefeated and

No. 1-ranked Kentucky Wildcats. Any thoughts I have right now that aren't about how we can prepare for Kentucky are a complete waste of my time and energy.

How often do we all find ourselves in this situation? It's so easy to get distracted and turn your attention to things that you either can't do anything about or things that won't make any difference in whether you accomplish your long-term goals.

If you allow yourself to lose track of the big picture and get distracted by things that are out of your control, you'll never achieve your dreams.

Your actions and results will always follow your thoughts. That's why you have to be disciplined about the thoughts you choose to focus on.

Anything that causes you to worry or stew about things you have no control over is a distraction. A distraction is just another negative influence that must be cut loose.

These distractions come in all forms and they whittle away at our grit. They distract us from the big picture—the dreams we originally set out to accomplish. They raise doubts, they confuse us, and they sap us of the energy we need to focus on what's actually important.

We have so many choices in this world, but those too can become a distraction. They can constantly make us question ourselves and wonder if "the grass is greener" elsewhere.

How do we keep ourselves focused on the things that actually matter?

Here's a simple equation that cuts through the noise and ensures that you stay focused on the right things:

E + R = O

The E stands for Events. The R stands for Responses. And the O stands for Outcomes.

You can't do anything about the E's. These are things that have already happened or things that may happen in the future that you have no control over.

The R's are what you do have control over. No matter what Events happen to you, you always have total control over how you Respond to those Events.

How you Respond to an Event is what determines your Outcome.

Most people spend all their time worrying about E's, which they can do nothing about. On the other hand, the happiest and most successful people spend their time and energy focusing on the R's, which they completely control.

Whenever you find yourself stewing or worrying, stop and ask yourself if you're focusing on an E or an R. If it's an E, you have to mentally throw it away. That's a distraction, something that will knock you off course and get in the way of you achieving your goals.

Then, you must shift your focus immediately to an R. "Okay, it happened, now what am I going to do about it?"

This works just as well when worrying about future Events as it does past Events. "Okay, *if* it happens, what am I going to do about it?"

This simple equation has saved me often in life. It's saving me right now. As I write this, I realize that I'm sitting on a plane and focusing on an E that I can do nothing about. No more of that! I'm now shifting my focus to an R. I will write a statement for the press explaining the reason for my retirement and that I will not be answering questions about it until after the season because I want this week to be about our players and our university, not me. I will respectfully request that players not be asked questions about my retirement either.

And that will be that. I've decided on an R that should positively affect our Outcome.

Refer to that simple equation throughout your life. It will ensure that you focus on your big-picture goals and don't get distracted by things you can do nothing about.

Now that that's done, I need to shift my focus to another important R.

How will our team Respond to the top-ranked and undefeated Kentucky Wildcats? They're one of the most talented teams ever assembled. That's the E that we can't change. All we can control is the R, our game plan for them.

Rule No. 12
Don't Waste a Day

"Champions do not become champions when they win an event, but in the hours, weeks, months, and years they spend preparing for it. The victorious performance itself is merely a demonstration of their championship character."
MICHAEL JORDAN, NBA Champion basketball player

Sunday, April 4, 2015
Indianapolis, Indiana

How did we do it? How did we go up against Kentucky—a team loaded with future NBA players, a team that started the season ranked No. 1 in the nation, a team that held onto that No. 1 ranking all season long as it defeated 38-straight teams, and a team that the media said may be the most talented *ever*—how did we go up against this "unbeatable" team and pull off the upset of all upsets on Saturday night?

As I walked off the court following our victory, the sideline reporter for CBS asked me, "Coach, how did you do it? How did you knock off Kentucky?"

I answered truthfully, "One day, one practice, and one possession at a time."

We didn't beat Kentucky only on Saturday, April 3rd. We beat them back in the summer when our guys were putting in extra time conditioning. We beat them in the weight room with grueling workouts all year long. We beat them in November, December, and February, when we were battling through 13 defeats and learning lessons from each and every one of them.

We didn't win Saturday's game, 61-60, only because Marcus Madden hit his two free throws with 0.2 seconds left on the clock to give us our first lead of the game. We also won because DeAndre Jackson had four steals in the first five minutes of the game, because our center, Drew Henley, blocked the final two shots Kentucky took in the first half, and because our backup guard, Bobby Hill, dove for a loose ball and forced a jump ball and change of possession early in the second half.

We didn't beat Kentucky only because of our performance Saturday night; we beat them because of the hard work, study, sacrifice, and can-do attitude our players and coaches have put into this program for the decades leading up to this moment. It *all* led us to this victory.

My point is, no single play or single moment accomplishes anything of significance. **It's the little** things done right and done repeatedly over a long period of time that add up to big results.

Along with my *keep moving forward* mantra, my players constantly hear me say, "Don't waste a day."

It means that **every day, every practice, and every moment in your life is leading you towards something. Your effort and attitude *every day* will determine what that something is.**

Those who win the big game, hit the final shot, land the big sale, get the dream job, or earn the important degree; they don't achieve those things in one lucky moment. Those achievements result from hours, days, weeks, months, and years of hard work, optimism, discipline, continuous learning, and determination.

Ultimately, those who achieve the greatest accomplishments are those who waste the fewest days.

A few weeks ago, I wrote to you about the importance of creating your own destiny. I want to be clear that your destiny isn't determined in one moment of inspiration. It's determined by your *daily* effort over very long periods of time.

This is what grit is all about.

Anyone can be motivated to work hard and go after something for a day, a week, or a few months. But champions are motivated to work towards something each and every day for years and years.

I'm a competitive person. I love to compete in anything and everything. I'll never apologize for being a relentless competitor.

But some people have the wrong idea about what competition is. They think that competition is all about defeating someone else. They think competition is a zero-sum game with one person's success always coming at the expense of another person's failure.

But that's not what true competition is.

True competition is with yourself. It's about improving yourself each and every day. The competitor's goal is to get better every single day.

Pete Carroll, one of just three football coaches to win a college football national championship and a Super Bowl in pro football, likes to say that the essence of competition is to strive to do things better than they've ever been done before. I couldn't agree more.

And to do that, you must make it a *daily* goal to do things better and better.

Tomorrow night, we will play Duke for the NCAA Division 1 national championship. To most observers, we showed up "overnight" as one of the best basketball teams in the country. But the "overnight success" is a myth. Talk to any so-called overnight success and you'll find that years of preparation preceded their success. Talk to my players and coaches about our exhausting offseason workouts, our relentless commitment to positive self-talk, our hours and hours of team and individual practices and meetings, those long rides home after a loss and the bounce-back efforts that followed. Ask my seniors about the four years they put into this program *prior* to this point.

There's nothing "overnight" about what it takes to succeed.

Each day, you need to be moving just a little bit closer to your dream coming true. It won't happen all at once and it won't happen as quickly as you

wish. But it *will* happen if you refuse to waste a day.

I know this sounds like classic "coach talk," but it really is the little things that make the biggest difference. It's a focus on the fundamentals. It's a focus on the daily habits to do things the right way, again and again, that will determine whether you're successful.

I also know that we all have bad days from time to time. We all have days where we know we didn't honestly move forward, where we didn't inch closer to our dream coming true. This happens. Don't beat yourself up about it. But don't ignore it either.

Every night when you go to bed, do an honest evaluation of what you did during the day. Did you give your best effort? Did you keep a positive attitude or allow yourself to get cynical or apathetic? Did you learn something important? Did you follow through on your commitments? Did you do something to push yourself closer to your goals? If the answer is no, acknowledge it and promise to not waste tomorrow. If the answer is yes, be proud of yourself and promise to not waste tomorrow.

Every single day is a crucial opportunity for you to get closer to becoming the person you want to be. Don't waste that opportunity. Don't waste a day.

Rule No. 13
Life Is a Series of Wins and Lessons

"I've learned that something constructive comes from every defeat."

TOM LANDRY, Super Bowl Champion football coach

Earlier this evening, we played our guts out in the national championship game against Duke. I wish I could tell you that our Cinderella season had a storybook ending. I wish I could tell you that my players ended the night hoisting the national championship trophy. I wish I could tell you that the last image of me as a college basketball coach was cutting down the net and celebrating a third national championship in Indianapolis.

But, that's not what happened. When the final buzzer sounded, the Blue Devils had defeated St. Rita's, 68-64.

We played a great game tonight, we truly did. But Duke played better. They made more plays than we did. Period. We had the lead with four minutes left in the game, but Coach Mike Krzyzewski led his team back and he won his fifth national title at Duke.

That's part of life. Sometimes you give everything you've got and you still fall short of your goal...at least in the short term.

But one thing I learned long ago is that there isn't a single disappointment in life that doesn't serve as an opportunity to learn something important. Life isn't a series of wins and losses; it's a series of wins and *lessons*. Whether it's losing a game, losing a job, going through a health crisis, going through a financial crisis, or losing someone close to you, there is *always* a lesson to be learned if you look for it.

I believe that's ultimately the purpose of this life: to learn. To learn how to become a better person. To learn the skills and values that make you happier and more successful.

Within every loss—of any kind—there is a crucial lesson you're supposed to learn.

I believe that with all my heart.

It could be a lesson in humility—that is, learning to set a good example by accepting setbacks with class. It could be a lesson in getting your priorities straight and recognizing what is most important in life. It could be a lesson in courage—learning to face a failure head-on and not let fear keep you from trying again. It could be a lesson that you don't understand until years later when you look back and see how a setback led you down a new path, made you a stronger person, gave you an experience that you were able to use to help someone else, or set you up for a greater success much later.

When you look for the lesson in every loss or setback, you'll avoid wallowing in defeat or self-pity and you'll bounce back quickly. You'll never feel like a setback was all for nothing. You'll see it as a learning opportunity, an opportunity to learn something that could never be fully learned in victory.

That's the truth, whether we like hearing it or not.

At its core, every valuable lesson is a lesson in grit. Life has a way of teaching us—again and again—that we must keep persevering. We must keep moving forward. We must never back down.

What lesson can my team learn from the loss to Duke? Well, it will be different for everyone involved. Our players and coaches will likely take away lessons much different than the lesson I'm supposed to learn from it.

For me, I think the lesson tonight is one of gratitude. It's easy to be gracious and thankful when everything is going your way. Though my final game as a coach ended in defeat, I looked up in the stands afterwards and saw so many people who care deeply about me.

My wife, Mary Lou, was there cheering as she always does. She made so many sacrifices to support me through the years. I owe that woman everything.

I saw our children in the stands along with several of you grandkids. It warmed my heart to see you all there, cheering on my final day at the office.

I saw many former players and colleagues with tears in their eyes as they applauded our team's final effort.

I saw thousands of fans who have supported our program through the decades.

So much love, so much support, even in defeat. What more can a man ask for?

I've had an extraordinary career doing something I've loved to do. Would I have preferred to go out with a victory instead of a defeat? You better believe it! But would I trade any of my previous 42 seasons as head coach at St. Rita's for a different result tonight? Not a chance in hell.

I'm thankful for this moment. I truly am.

Woody Hayes, the legendary Ohio State football coach, once said, "There's nothing that cleanses your soul like getting the hell kicked out of you." That quote always gets a chuckle, but I think what I'm feeling tonight is something like what Coach Hayes was referring to.

If you can be grateful and feel good about the job you've done, the life you have, and the people around you even in the face of a heartbreaking defeat on your last day on the job; then that makes you a champion in life.

That's what it truly means to go out on top.

Rule No. 14
Don't Put Off
Pursuing Your Dreams

"Live every day as if it's your last because someday you're going to be right."

MUHAMMAD ALI, World Heavyweight Champion boxer

Monday, April 12, 2015
Kansas City, Missouri

It's the Monday after our season has ended and the finality of it all is sinking in. After 43 seasons of running a basketball program, I will never coach another team. Not only that, but I will now turn my attention to what will *potentially* be a much more significant final chapter—that is, the final chapter of my life.

With everything going on over the past month, I never really had a chance to face the seriousness of cancer and the fact that my time on this earth is possibly running out much faster than I imagined.

When you face these final chapters of life—whether it be the end of a career or the end of life itself—I suppose it's only natural to look back and wonder about things you wish you would have done differently. It now occurs to me that not writing these letters sooner is one of the regrets I have.

But just like any other disappointment, you can find valuable life lessons in your regrets.

When I first sat down to write you, I didn't think it would stretch on quite so long. I realize now I've written a pile of letters that could serve as a small book. I suppose this is my little instruction manual for how to live a successful life.

Seeing the final result of this book makes me realize that I should have written this much sooner.

For years, I had publishers asking me to write a book. I have a passion for reading and therefore always loved the idea of writing a book. It had always been a dream of mine to write something that would outlast me. But, I kept putting off that dream. I had a new excuse each season. I kept finding a reason to think that *next* season would be the year to do it.

And now, there won't be a next season for me.

This brings me to another crucial rule for life: **Don't put off the pursuit of your dreams.**

Most people have dreams in their heart that they keep putting off for "someday." They say they will pursue their dream when they have more money in the bank, when the kids have grown up, when the mortgage is paid, when things settle down at work, when they retire, when they finish the move, on and on this list goes. There's always a "someday" out there when they say they'll stop putting off their dream and start pursuing it.

But, that "someday" never comes and they leave this life with a dream still in their heart.

Don't let that be you. There's nothing more disappointing than wasted potential. It's so sad to think about all the things that could've been if someone had only had the courage to follow the dreams in their heart.

Time catches up with all of us and if you don't pursue your dreams now, your "someday" may never come.

While writing a book is a dream that I put off way too long, I can proudly say that I pursued my dream of being a basketball coach with everything I had. And yes, there were times when I questioned whether I had what it takes to continue doing it for another season. Changing times brought new challenges every year. I heard all the naysayers saying I should be fired. But I followed the rules I'm sharing with you to overcome those challenges. And I thank God that I did. I thank God that these rules were instilled in me.

I'm not going to sugarcoat it. Chasing a big dream *will* force you to encounter big obstacles along the way. But it's worth it. The journey *is* worth it.

Please trust me on this one.

Rule No. 15
Don't Quit.
Don't Ever Quit

"You're never a loser until you quit trying."

MIKE DITKA, Super Bowl champion football coach

Sunday, April 18, 2015
Kansas City, Missouri

Tomorrow morning, I will begin a new season. This time, my opponent is cancer. I've always tried to live my life by walking in faith and not dwelling on fear. Whenever faced with a difficult decision, I've tried to choose faith over fear. Courage is an important aspect of grit and sometimes it takes blind faith to get your courage up.

But I'll be completely honest with you, I'm fearful about my cancer treatment. I'm scared about whether it will be successful in wiping out the cancer and extending my life. I'm also fearful about how painful the treatment will be as I've heard numerous horror stories and I've had enough conversations with my doctors that started out with, "I'll be completely honest with you, Bob, this isn't going to be pleasant."

It's okay to admit your fears. It's disingenuous to ignore your fears and pretend you're not afraid when you really are. **Recognizing your fear is the first step towards conquering that fear.**

How does one conquer their fears? Simple.

First, you make the decision to not complain about it. Some fears cannot be avoided and if that's the case, complaining about them won't make them go away. Instead, it will only make them worse.

Secondly, you must not blame others for what you have to face. Even if whatever you're facing really is someone else's fault, it wastes your time and energy to sit around blaming them for where you are now. Blaming others won't do a thing to alleviate your fear. Blame weakens *you*, not the person you're blaming. Even worse, when you start blaming someone else for where you are—whether the blame is warranted or not—it becomes too easy to start passing the blame to other people for other problems as well. Don't do it. As soon as you hear yourself blaming others for your problems, stop it immediately and start asking yourself: "What am I going to do about it?"

And finally, the final step in conquering your fear is to make the decision that you will *never* give up.

You must make an ironclad contract with yourself that you will not retreat and you will never stop fighting. All you can do is promise yourself that even if you go down, you'll go down swinging.

This rule—to *never* give up—is the final rule I have to share with you. This rule is the foundation of the previous fourteen rules. It's the very essence of grit.

A lot of people today have the wrong idea about what makes a person successful. They like to think that someone is born into success. But that's not how it works. **Nobody can give you success. It has to be earned.**

I really don't know what to expect in the months to come. I don't know how many days I have left in this world and that's a scary thing to consider. At the same time, I suppose nobody truly knows how much time they have left.

With that in mind, I'd like to leave you with this final thought.

No matter what happens to you in life, please don't ever forget this: **The successful person is not the person who goes through life and makes the** fewest mistakes. The successful person is the person who is willing to make mistakes, over and over, and keep getting back up to try again. The successful person is the one who gets knocked down nine times, but gets up ten times.

The successful person is the one who never, *ever*, quits. That's what it means to have grit.

If you embrace that attitude, you will achieve success beyond your wildest dreams. I guarantee it.

The only thing that can stop you in life is you.

Don't complain, don't blame, and don't *ever* quit on your dreams.

That's what it means to be gritty. And that's what it means to be successful.

Your Proud and Loving Grandfather,
Bob Flanagan

About the Author

DARRIN DONNELLY is an author and entrepreneur. He and his products have been featured in publications such as *The Wall Street Journal*, *Sports Illustrated*, *Fast Company Magazine*, and newspapers, websites, and radio outlets all over the world. He lives in Kansas City with his wife and three children.

Donnelly can be reached at: *SportsForTheSoul.com*

Sports for the Soul

This book is part of the *Sports for the Soul* series. For updates on this book, a sneak peek at future books, and a free newsletter that delivers powerful advice and inspiration from top coaches, athletes, and sports psychologists, join us at: **SportsForTheSoul.com**.

The *Sports for the Soul* newsletter will help you:

- Find your purpose and follow your passion
- Use a positive mental attitude to achieve more
- Build your self-confidence
- Develop mental toughness
- Increase your energy and stay motivated
- Harness the power of positive self-talk
- Explore the spiritual side of success
- Be a positive leader for your family and your team
- Become the best version of yourself
- And much more…

Join us now at **SportsForTheSoul.com**.

Don't miss Book No. 1 of the *Sports for the Soul* series:

Think Like a Warrior
by Darrin Donnelly

In this inspirational fable, Chris McNeely is a college football coach who is at the end of his rope after a hard-and-fast fall from the top of his profession. Now bankrupt and on the verge of losing his job, he has no idea what he's doing wrong or how to get back on track.

Angry, worried, and desperate for help, Chris receives mysterious visits from five of history's greatest coaches: **John Wooden, Buck O'Neil, Herb Brooks, Bear Bryant, and Vince Lombardi**. Together, these five legendary leaders teach Chris how to "think like a warrior" and take control of his life. The "warrior mindset" he develops changes his life forever — and it will change yours as well.

Made in the USA
Columbia, SC
13 November 2019